I am
fearfully
& wonderfully made.

Psalm 139:14

God is always ready to help.

Psalm 46:1

Trust in the Lord with all your heart.

Proverbs 3:5

CHILDREN ARE A GIFT FROM THE LORD.

PSALM 127:3

The Lord is my shepherd;
I have all that I need.

Psalm 23:1

The Lord has done
amazing things for us!
What joy!
Psalm 126:3

The earth is the Lord's, and everything in it.

Psalm 24:1

Praise the Lord.

Psalm 150:6

God is the King
of all the earth.
Psalm 47:7

Best friends forever!

Two people are better off than one,
   for they can help each other succeed. Ecclesiastes 4:9

Bloom where God plants you!

In the beginning God created the heavens and the earth. Genesis 1:1

Let your light shine.

Matthew 5:16

The Lord
is good!
His love will
last forever.
Psalm 100:5

We live by **faith**, not by what we see.

2 Corinthians 5:7

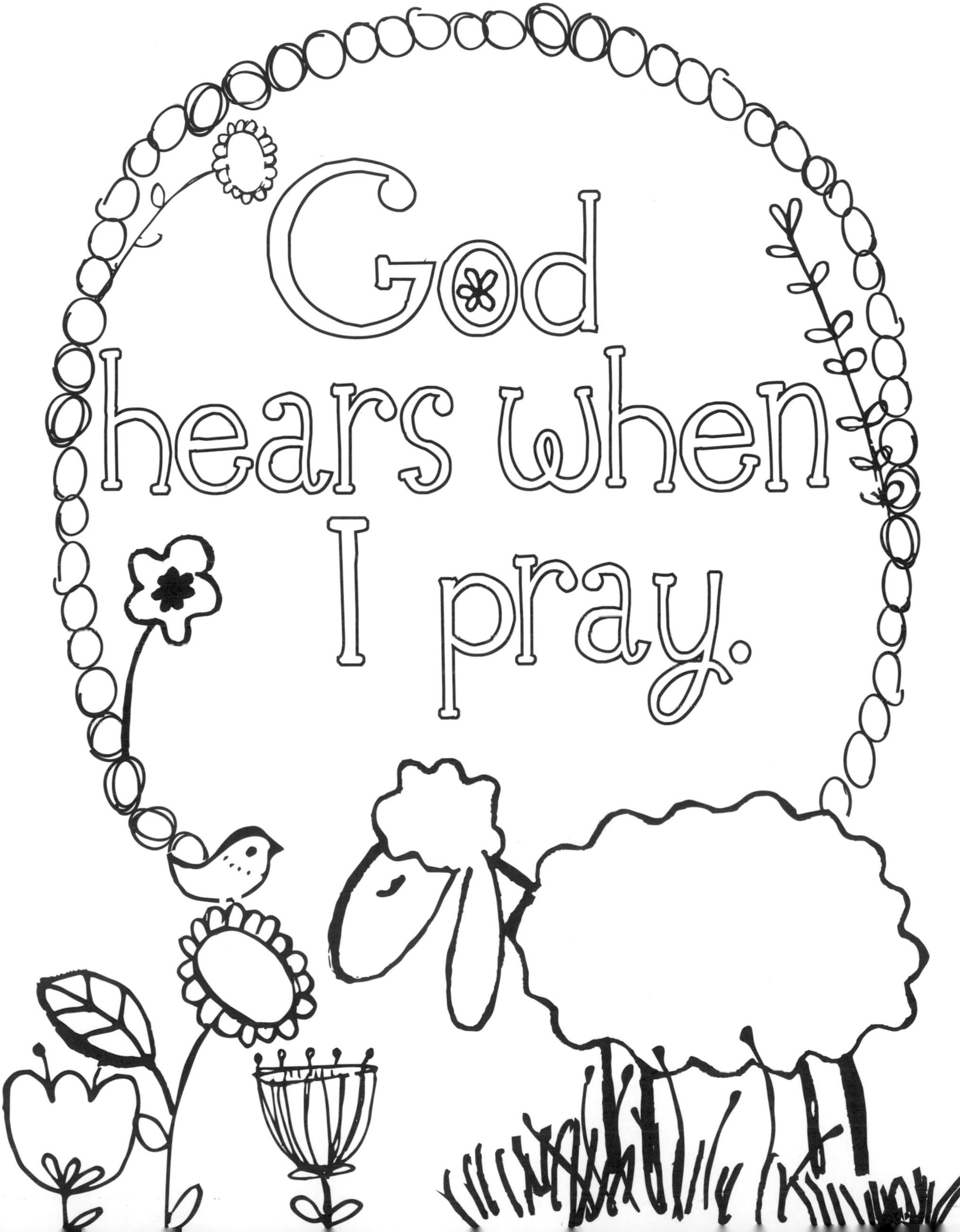
God hears when I pray.

Be joyful!

Trust God.

Love always.

Sing for joy!

BEST *mom* EVER

You are special to God.

To my best friend

JESUS LOVES YOU!

Bloom where
God plants
you!

Cards
to color and cut

God cares for you.
1 Peter 5:7

I love you!

Have a HAPPY day!

Rejoice
in the Lord.

Philippians 4:4

You
are
precious
and
loved.

Shine
for
Jesus!